The Tree Surgeon's Gift

Scripta Humanistica

Directed by
BRUNO M. DAMIANI
The Catholic University of America

ADVISORY BOARD

The Tree Surgeon's Gift

Edward C. Lynskey

𝕾cripta 𝕳umanistica

69

Lynskey, Edward C.
   The tree surgeon's gift / Edward C. Lynskey.
      p. cm. — (Scripta Humanistica : 69)
   ISBN 0-916379-75-2 : $22.50
   I. Title. II. Series: Scripta Humanistica (Series) ; 69.
   PS3562.Y44486T7   1990
   811'.54—dc20   90-8572
                                                                      CIP

                            Publisher and Distributor:
                            SCRIPTA HUMANISTICA
                               1383 Kersey Lane
                         Potomac, Maryland 20854 U.S.A.

For Heather
with all new love,
and sweet old affection

Acknowledgments

Grateful acknowledgment is made to the following journals in which these poems, or earlier versions of them, have appeared:

Abbey, Amelia, America, American Poetry Review, The Atlantic Monthly, Antigonish Review, Apalachee Quarterly, Baltimore Sun Magazine, Ball State University Forum, Blue Unicorn, Cape Rock Journal, Carolina Quarterly, College English, Cotton Boll/Atlanta Review, Four Quarters, Greenfield Review, Greensboro Review, Hawaii Review, Hiram Poetry Review, The Hollins Critic, Hampden-Sydney Review, Kansas Quarterly, Manhattan Poetry Review, Mid-American Review, Minnesota Review, The National Forum, Negative Capability, New Mexico Humanities Review, The New Renaissance, Now and Then, Outerbridge, Paintbrush, Pembroke Magazine, Poetry Now, Poem, Pulpsmith, Poet Lore, River Styx, Southern Humanities Review, Southern Poetry Review, Southwest Review, St. Anthony's Messenger, Texas Review, University of Windsor Review, Visions, Washington Review, Windless Orchard, and *Webster Review.*

"Bad Apples" appeared in *Lost Beat and Broke in Milwaukee Anthology.* Ed. Jesse Glass, Jr. (Milwaukee: Goethe's Notes, 1986).

"The Tree Surgeon's Alibi" appeared in *Suicide Notes: An Anthology.* Ed. Christine A. Willis. (Troy, New York, 1987).

"If He Hollers, Let Him Go" appeared in *The Best of Spitball Magazine Anthology.* Ed. Mike Shannon. (New York: Harper & Row, 1990).

"Mechanized Dreams" appeared in *Anthology of Magazine Verse.* Ed. Alan Pater. (Los Angeles: Monitor Books, 1987).

The following poems appeared in the chapbook *Teeth of the Hydra.* (Washington, D.C.: Crop Dust Press, 1986): "Teeth of the Hydra," "The Tree Surgeon's Gift," "The Risk of Green," "Fallen Angels," "Inside the Gun Factory," and "Winter Fields: Getting Through."

Table of Contents

Part III — Places

Part IV — Biography

Foreword

Speaking Plainly

The virtues of plain speaking in poetry perhaps have never been so thoroughly touted as in the present decades. But it still remains difficult to find true poets speaking plainly. What we mostly find are academics writing in borrowed tough-guy idiom or deep-dipped Romantics who have simply turned a romantic style inside out.

But poets who respect subject matter taken from ordinary daily life, from familiar affections and disorders, from homely locales and manual labor, and who speak at all opportunity straight to the point are as rare as. . . Well, as rare as Joseph Langland and E. A. Robinson and Hugh MacDiarmuid and Richard Hugo.

The fact of this rarity might point toward the cooler fact that our vaunted admiration for plain speaking is mostly lip service. Or it might point toward the fact that plainspoken poems are hard to write, requiring gifts less ornate but as large as those required by romantic and metaphysical poets.

Edward C. Lynskey's "Barthlomew's Cobbler" begins with a few lines that seem to serve merely to place a situation within a solidly observed setting.

Next door the closed vinegar works the smudgy
cobbler is caught late in the bleary panes
dressing his shopfront, punching and stitching
oily leather—he gestures at me to come the hell
inside out the sleet.

That's the opening: as deft and economical and gritty in intention as any naturalistic short story. It is easy to imagine an unaccustomed reader asking in all innocence, "But where is the poetry?" Not seeing at first that the cobbler's gesture gives us the whole character and flavor of his speech, the actual sound of his talk, even though he hasn't yet uttered a word.

So that we are prepared for the cobbler's sentence in the final lines, words with their own store of unwary innocent suggestiveness:

> Cracking the thin soles, the cobbler tells me
> a boy-soldier needs tough leather to get through boot camp.

Edward C. Lynskey has given the force of his fine talent, and the strong faith of his poetry, to the people of this world, the world we think we know. It has richly rewarded him with poems. And the poems bountifully reward his readers. Because, as we now begin to see, we didn't really know the ordinary world at all, not at all.

—Fred Chappell

I
Relationships

The Lame Shall Enter First

His favorite of seven
daughters, I nursed the old man,
dogridden and bedtired and soon
to die. His combative lungs
wheezed as a pair of leaky
bellows. I wondered at how those eyes
talked, gesturing, restless as wrens
inside Tom Cat's yard. I turned the
pages of the family Bible; he seldom
strayed from Esdras: so much depends on
asylum, offered in thick woods,
hollows in the tidewrack. His mind
snatched four words in the space
God had permitted for one. He
sensed the lateness of summer: the smell of mown
vetch, the fence of wet sheets,
spired by a clothespole, slapping in a burst
of breeze. And in the stillbirth of the midnight,
he dreamt, God yes, dammit he did:
burning decks at sea; howling coves
along Dolly Sods; distressing faces in mirrors.
His eyes sank, looking like chalky
taws, and I knew it wasn't the last
breath that undid him, but all those
unnoticed which had gone before it.

Lights Over Quantico, USMC

Summer's lazy axis I think elucidated best my
father's psyche: getting through the brief but
hot nights, he'd slump over the airy panes, cut
his bloodshot eyes toward the hushed and distant
margins of the Corps' timber. Did he grieve alone
for his choice made to slumber in a powdery boudoir,
dreaming of a carbine and a hammock to sling against Ché?

The sentry in him read the starry horizons, paused
at the roof over the Quantico garrison. In that land
leathernecks fresh back from the Mekong River concocted
an argosy of combustible rockets, pissed enough to shoot
them high up the very bowels of Heaven itself, remembering
the rainbow infernos replete with deafening swirls. For
my sake he acted like the phantasmagoric lights were

something wrong with the steamy sferics of late June
clashing with the wintry remnants of April. He called
me a fortunate son, perhaps, for rarely were the night
lights witnessed but by a few insomniacs. Even now after
this long night since, my father's searching gaze will
shine in dreams. I watch the enigmatic lights and fall
silent, never singing as he did of foreign shores and halls.

Turnip Patch Kids

Black Maria chided us children to keep
off the burial plots of her relations,
lords of sleep you let be or else they
breathed on you, turning your dreams bad.
Limestones were tucked under their derbies,
rolled beneath their shoes. Evenings clouds
blew free firespit stars. Maria slipped on her nervy
red wrap, pattered quickly outback, silver
snake bracelets and belted church keys
jangling bloodkin ghosts she knew not by mug,
nor by stature, mostly from the stories handed
her. Spading up a circle, she raised turnips,
radishes in the good earth, uprooting tubers
smooth as kewpie dolls, blessed by her people,
offered us to eat raw with lick salt. The leafy
tops she boiled down to a sickly green to feed
babies, crying for mothers gone to teapot socials.
At the start of winter, we used to steal
away to the fenceless graveyard to stand smack
middle of Black Maria's whole world we wanted for ours.

The Night Light

Fresh breezes through the patchy piedmont stir
cedar switches to scratch the tin roof,
like whisks of straw from the coo witch's
broom swooping low to fetch all tired souls.
A girl pumps her father's consumptive lungs;
her throat tightens as do pythons about the sleeping

mongoose. She nurses his running sores with styptic
webs, pours coal oil in the ingle sputtering to
animate the room where electricity isn't permitted.
Maduro tobacco fails its office and she unstoppers
sniffing salts to spell his bad dreams and broken
sleep. The Milky Way becomes a cowpath she drifts

down with her father, pleasuring to see him mend
fence and mow vetch. Back then he'd been quick to
laugh how he'd wind up in Hell pumping thunder,
by Jezebel, at three cents a clap. The girl hears his
rasping cough, steps lightly into his room carrying
the coal-oil lamp. She leans over the open mouth, softly
blows out the wick of his tongue; the room goes dark.

Lillian's Chair

She sits awry on the backstoop, counterpane
draped around her knock-knees, her eyes
closed. Like a crippled De Soto, she has been towed
here to fall apart. Descending dusk brings out
mosquito hawks gone mad over the orchard,
where our voices trail low and sawdusty, forming
words that she snatches. Come April, now, Lillian
shall try the creaks in her bones, draw a bellows'
breath and, murmuring "the quince needs seeing after,"
rise up like Lady Lazarus, drifting down
to the lichen-smitten stone wall, heading far
afield, borne largely by her own convictions.
And as always happens, we will return from walking
late, ready to greet her, lame legs less apparent now
in the blanketing darkness. And we will grieve alone,
finding Lillian's chair empty, left rocking on the stoop.

Windless Orchards

I'd thought I had forgotten the fresh
lyrics of spring but it all came back
again tonight. I woke to a rain pelting
upstairs on the tin roof like a mad tinker
come to bang his wares. I stood agape
before the flashing panes while the long storm
passed me by. Showers in April can turn
lovers out of sorts, wild and cold drops
spattering on the still, naked limbs of windless
orchards. Once on a country road in April,
far off, we were soaked by a sudden drench,
and ran to fall together inside a barn. Her small
shaking body was warm, God it was that, my gypsy
bathed in the straw's bonfire. But tonight could
have been any one of a hundred times and places.
Rains like every boy who has ever hurt in love,
crying all at once, and all the tears running today
through my memory of a young girl in a far country.

Bad Apples

In the palm of his soul, my father saw
wheelbarrows toppled with yellow
apples picked from the orchard by his sons.
We'd hustle fruit to the cold-storage shed,
sorting them inside wooden crates
stenciled with the family name Peterbilt
diesels spread throughout the Tri-State.
Buffing thick skin, he held up one Rome,
laughing with his health alive in his
eyes gleaming like foxfire in the wilderness.

Each spring we dibbled home the seedlings,
trying to make the truck farm produce
before the old man's lungs quit. Broken on his
back, he wished for the emperor's orchard,
four decades long refused to appear.
I think about him now ruminating,
hunched near the frost-flowered pane,
looking outwardly for his mound to grow,
learning slowly to hate the taste of apples.

The Hyacinth Girl
(for Alma T. Stocking — 1909-1990)

Yesterday's letter from her might have opened:
"Ides of March. Sunny. Southerly breezes today.
Mercury 74°F, climbing." She cultivated gentle
paths colored by forsythia falling as yellow
founts, hydrangea touching the panes, crepe myrtle
bordering fencerows. People out on rainy days nodded

at her red hyacinths growing beneath ancient oaks
lifting clouds. Those later years she survived her
circle of kin and filled her long days with April's gentle
blooms. Neighbors called to marvel at the hyacinths
she fetched from wet gardens; she offered fragrant boughs
even today daughters remember as alive and beautiful.

When winter's cold axis turned to spring, she passed
away asleep, her peaceful journey south. The gardens were
cut for rental property. April her true colors showed
again: snowdrop narcissus, buttery jonquil, painterly
iris, and set against the porch as if pressed from wax,
stirring in a gentle breeze were healing, red hyacinths.

Pink Flamingos

Pink flamingos are down
for the night, snickering
in the savannahs, primping
rouge and feather, peeping
under tucked wings to the St.
Cyr shore. I live there in a
tin can shack, bumming
beaches for what piece of
eight Edward Teach tumbles
ashore. I smoke alone beneath
the menstrual moon, hung
in a pecan grove like a
lantern lit by a sleepy rube.

I dreamed half my
life of flying north to
Charleston. But I ended up
riveting steel plate on
lobster shifts. This job
gets under my collar until
I toot up at six. Pink
flamingos fall down for
the night, snickering again
back the marsh when I lean
to the moon who fills
me with her hairy seed.

Kiss of Kin

Came my father's people (rumored to be
white trash) spewed out of Pittsburgh's
cold slag furnaces. Over and down
the ancient humps of the Alleghenies
the succeeding generations wandered, a litmus
dipped in the local wood economies gone
bust: Winchester's obsolete wheelwrights,

cabinetmaker's sons bankrupt by Staunton,
turpentine works in Marion set to torch.
By car I try to reach back and connect with the
remote family boneyards strung down the valley
like laundry left hanging in rain. Touching
their terse bloodlines carved in the mossy-
back slabs of native limestone, I think sadly
back on their ages lame with polio, body

minerals gleaned from the clay they ingested;
the love they matched on straw ticks, rustling
as the burst of breeze that tumbled one
great-grandfather to Lynchburg, looking for his
family livelihood to tend the piedmont loam,
plowing deep furrows for tobacco in the employ
of Mister R. J. Reynolds, erecting his house
out of brick and tin where I kiss his kin, my kin.

Polio Summers

All those summers you lived sitting
on wire-spoked wheels to negotiate
hallways and go out on the deck. Starry
nights you bested the Egyptians figuring
the apogees of the eight sister planets,
grew to make a sense how an inscrutable God,
psychic in the whole upstairs of space,
might roll a compensating grace to the lame, spin
straw into an army's bullion to fight wars.
I remember telling you bedside how a kid
crawled through melons and cukes to capture
a garter snake inside a jar, and you
asked to see it with your wonderful grey
eyes that charmed the serpent into coiling,
cooing submission. Your fortitude to ride out
winter planted in an iron lung, shockingly
beyond any physician's prognosis, bought me
time in June to understand about death.

II
Rituals

The Tree Surgeon's Gift

What he liked best was freewheeling
high across the windless dome
of a treetop, his guy ropes flailing
like the smashed strands
of a mad spider's webbing.

When the "uptown mugwumps" voted
to uproot the Hang Tree
from the public garden, he didn't
kick. His crew did the work:
setting to torch the high branches.

He placed its heartwood
in the soft jaws of the Le Blond lathe,
crafting a lamp post.
By bulb light he studied
the dark lines of the hangman.

The Risk of Green

Today it'll rain while I work
the upper branches of a beech,
bark worn as ancient coins.
The squaw wood needs thinning,
back to the foliage around my
throat flapping clean as baby linen.
I remember meeting a man once
who sat in his garden, amongst
the nasturtiums and melons,
a newspaper folded beneath
his elbow like the wounded wing
of a crow. His was a heart attack
victim's pastime in earnest.
Rain's come and I'll not
back down; I'll hold to the tree,
an angel tumbled that far,
willing to take the risk of green.

Shade Tree Mechanics

My father always stood behind his daddy's brass
tack saying that the hog-block engines need
special treatment, handling with gentle persuasion
like tickling memories left from the old days.
Fumbling beneath the flipped hood with the big car's

inner workings, they looked to know its idiosyncrasies,
what fatal leaks the droplight illuminated, their hands
feeling the horsepower's mounting throb in the carburetor.
When those two got together, they conspired to practice
the voodoo of car repairs, excitable kids rocking on

their haunches, gesturing with broke matchsticks,
reinventing toothed gears and slambang pistons,
etched in the coal cinders out front the rickety
garage, jawing for hours on the cubic virtues of the
slant-head eight, tongues unerring as the mosquito hawks

flapping about their ears. And like them with my hands
buried deep in crankcases, I too was initiated
to the hot, black lady called auto mechanics. Even
now years later what I like best are evenings tinkering
on my Olds, recalling with affection my father in greasy

bibs jacking up the front end beneath the shade
spread by a chinaberry tree, whistling looney tunes,
scooting crablike under the stilted chassis on a sack,
disappearing with a clutch of bright chromium tools
while I watched for the car to submit to his expert ways.

Inside the Gun Factory

The smell of cutting oil
and the machine noises butcher
the senses. I run the gun
lathe, drilling barrels mated
to frames in final assembly:
a revolver is born today.
The run-out is within tolerance.
I soak the barrel in varsol.
This job gets under your collar
and uses your head like a revolver.

Guns lend me some credence,
brighter than figs, cylinders
oily to spin easy, long ashy
sights open. The first thief
we turn to for nothing except measured
curses. Believe me, a Luger
snub-nose offers a better
defense against worlds filled
with pain. I left mine at home,
stuffed in the keyhole, ready
to bark at my hairy touch.

Seasons of the Hunter

Off work on that dim eve of Epiphany, my father
unslung his pump-action Fox to teach me the delicate
dynamics of safety and trigger, how the loud
report issued from firing, how it would whistle
inside your ears for days, and how sore your shoulder
felt from its mean kick. Pulling on camouflaged
khaki heavy with ammunition, he took me out back
into the freezing drizzle, schooling me
how seasoned huntsmen sense their game and go after it.
We crossed the sunken road and traveled far

afield, spooking the soybean stubble with our
boots. All at once the quail flushed, hollering for
mercy. I swung up the 16-gauge cannon, barking
birdshot into their ranks scattered already way beyond
range, the ejected shells pissing and steaming in the red
mire. We finished our trek that day not talking much,
walking home alongside fencerows smelling of cold
and of shaggy cedars, my father's stuffed bib
smeared with bloody bird entrails, their twiggy
feet sticking out, and my canvas bag limp and clean.

The Duck Corps Rupture

Peculiar the way mallards we unload
shotguns on wheel forever on in their antic
grace: flying in busted arcs, disrupted
parabolas, and lazy zigs over field and stream.
Something lovely keeps them airborne,
suspended high over souls, following
their fluttery relief cracked between the double
barrel's bead, silhouetted against the salmon
twilight, their wings always beating
us at the base of hairy trigger fingers.
We crouch smoking in the pit blind edging the
sump and hearing honks, spring up pumping,
the ejected shells stinging our cold cheeks,
shoulders banged sore, watching in disbelief
at pin feathers spilling down our hot, heaving breaths.
Those hunts I recall better when drunk or while
dreaming; I can see the faraway paths of ghostly
ducks winging on out, looking like they'd
never once taken a hit, weaving in the end over
our rough, winding roads going nowhere.

After Berrypicking

Those vinegary afternoons when others prefer sleep she
slips the latch, starts running to her late father's
fields banked by brilliant cockscomb. All the land
seems murmuring, breathing some sort of brazen
song, for it's here in late summer she loves
to venture. Alongside a fencerow unfit for
cultivation, left to lie rotting and rank, the heavy
vines sag over stone walls like fishnets. The girl stands,
loosens her braids to let fly her hair and, statuesque
in chemise, she picks thimbles from the bramble,
tipping her milk pails with the musky fruit. Dripping
its liquor down, a garter snake becomes drunk, threading
its weave through the hedge. She sees the snake eyes
cloudy with bad spells and crushes the spearhead
beneath her barefeet. Feasting in the sun the blue-
black juices, an alluring rouge, smear her mouth and
dribble down to streak her breasts as chalk
pigments, so ecstatic in their natural light. Feeling a dusky
torpor, she treks to home and bed, tired but not undone,
bearing in buckets her father's gifts to survive the summer.

Never Once

I'd awaken to hear you rustling alone
underneath the basement stairs,
piling our wash, limp and soused
bundles, into an orange crate to
carry atop your head upstairs into
the yard, bright as melons. You'd hang
our skins shed that week to flip and flap
until they were bone dry to gather at day's
end. The baby's linen you'd always
string in front of ours, the clothesline
spired to keep the clean garments from
draggling in the miry footpath. You'd
put up our leggings and underclothes
silhouetted between the thin muslin sheets.
Shirts with embroidered collars
were pinned up by their tails, the cuffs
rolled down, flailing after you in a burst
of breeze. Breeches dangled with the pockets
pulled out, akin to elephant ears. Never once
do I remember, in all the summers we passed,
your leaving the laundry hanging overnight.

Storm Windows

When the crooked goldenrods sag, when the wizened
asters nod, those floral gargoyles I swish by,
sleeping alongside piedmont roads going nowhere,
I shudder to feel September's nip creeping
up, late afternoon becoming bleary so soon
what with the tinselbugs doused, the crickets addled from
primitive frost. My thin shadow trudges across the yard:
"I do declare Delilah's little acre needs seeing after."
My neighbor cranks up his chainsaw, felling honey
locust trees, slinging sawdust, rattling chains,
stacking cordwood for fuel to grill his eggs in winter,
he tells me. I empty gutters, clean out the crepe
myrtles, store the screens in the cellar, dreading the last
chore. The ladder I lean against the house, mounting

the rungs to climb the beanstalk far up to the naked
sash where I pause on the sill to steady my vertigo.
I'm astonished to see that the shy pornographer wears a fuzzy
cap and granny glasses. Looking beyond the window,
how the counterpane is tucked back for rest, I can't
remember having dreamt it this way. A burst of breeze
knocks my knees, prodding me to get on with the real work.
I pull the storm window from the ground heavenwards,
reeling the tight twine clinched around its frame. I wrestle
with the heavy pane, fitting sides into tongued-grooves,
nailing the corners in place. I feel the sun's throttle
cold on my canvas back, knowing a full drummer's rot
the season to dodge wintry drafts has come home.

The Whore's Coo

Lying prone and smothered in moss, I
watched the prostitutes spilling out of the tool-
and-die works, walking solemnly down Taliaferro,
a mascara of tar, disinclined to advertise,
to advance themselves in the salmon flank
of morning. Huddled at the river's brink,
holding their sundresses high, they waded
unhurried in the dunking pools to attend
their morning toilettes: undoing hair
combed out in the wet breeze, sponging
each other with pumice and soap.

The grey light of dawn was lovely coming,
and I believed they would not mind me watching
from the opposite shore without announcement.
I did not tell them the Adventists sometimes
performed baptisms there where the suds fumed.
Nor did I ask them if they believed Mary
Magdalene soaped down daily to keep her
calling simon-pure. No, I remained silent
as their trespasses on the river ended;
and they withdrew, returning to their daybeds
too narrow for sleep, their sadness seemingly
untouched by the water passing close by me.

Choptank Oyster Dredgers

Yellow slickers flapping like broken wings,
watermen heave at hemp and pulley, hauling
out of the wet winds nets clattering with bone
china oysters. Chewing slow tobacco, they
shuck out the squibs, trolley the trashed
husks up-peninsula to farmers who, following Ruffin's
experimenting, apply crushed marl to the sour
clayloam to raise moneyed crops of tobacco that
hang from the rafters to cure in August heat.
Offseasons the oyster cribs are raked,
yielding sorry little, like waking
busted and bedded in Baltimore, astride one
fierce-faced whore, impotent. Others the watermen
knew, now dead, were watchers of the Chesapeake:
they learned her twisted lore, kept up on laughing
terms of intimacy, and knew the smells of impending
storm. Now the swollen, bad-bellied clouds
burst on the angered bay, catching again these
dredgers whose lot is neither oyster nor pearl.

Bartholomew's Cobbler

Next door the closed vinegar works the smudgy
cobbler is caught late in the bleary panes
dressing his shopfront, punching and stitching
oily leather — he gestures at me to come the hell
inside out the sleet. Without a civil greeting, he
faults the winter axis for ushering in streets
darkened before dinner, times not fit for working
white men. He jostles my ribs, shaking his shaggy
head, a riot laughing with me, judging people's
feet by their shoes cupped between his shinola
palms, mounting each of a pair on his anvil,
tapping on the bottoms with a tiny ball-peen hammer.
Hobs sticking out his lips, he waves me aside so as
not to screen the bulb light, points at my Spanish
boots with tooled snakes and roses on the counter.
The heels need rebuilding I say with Cat Paws,
rubber that dances all night on sudsy linoleum floors,
springs from the rain-slicked tarface in time to
thumb rides in fumey diesels headed to Waycross.
Cracking the thin soles, the cobbler tells me
a boy-soldier needs tough leather to get through boot camp.

End to Melancholy Questions

Winter long I read from the Book of Job
lit by kerosene, never slept more in my life.
"The Big Sleep" I called it. I made friends
with a lonely coyote, sharing tinned peaches.
I paced and ranted at my senses to pass a mad
winter in the ruined house north of where

the Soo Line died. My traps hung in the loft
because I refused to leave the sight of smoke
to skin a wolverine waiting with its steely jaws
sprung for me. Solitary others I knew living
on the tundra died from cold. Something inside
cracked. I stood at the south panes, watched

May's sun patch the forest, the great horned owl
hushed after a long night of melancholy questions.
The teakettle whistled on its fender, but I put on
my prairie coat to get out of the tarpaper shack.
Outside I felt the initial gusts in my dusty locks,
stirring warm and welcome as a new lover's breath.

The Tree Surgeon's Alibi

In the oak of the hangman, please
refrain from talk of rope,
a relic of a noose with seven
bloodknots that can snap the life out a
man's neck as a finger and thumb
snuff a burning wick that ages ago became
the swan song for spy, horse thief,
rogue. Not to fret about all that
now; it's just that cleaning squaw
wood from this height, my feet not
on firm soil, a crack of superstition
appears in my skull and tempted, I
peer down to see the alleged limb
stout as a man's thigh, its smooth
bark permitting braided hemp to hoist
up a sadsack of bones that God made.
On cue the body free falls like an
angel except he jerks and twists on
rope's end. Could I have been present,
I'd never confess to being the common
criminal first to curse at Christ. No,
I'd admit to sleeping in a stew outside
town and accept the sentence meted out: to
feel the slow choke of the hangman's rope.

Death of Cold

We loitered inside the stony ruins of a mansion,
standing around, coldcocked by a starry January
First ushering in buck season. Under the slab
chimney, the pine knots flapped fire, flapped
smoke, flapped out. We'd no money for kerosene but
the chewed off crimp from a shotgun shell sufficed.
The black powder hissed and then lit and we passed a
pilfered bottle of fine Crackling Rosie around for kicks.
We heated the yellow bricks, wadded them in sleeping
ticks and dragged them dreaming into steamy tropics.
At daybreak a black vet fresh from Vietnam cut by to
chance our ghost of smoke curling in the thin air:
"Come by the fire before you catch the death of cold."
His war stories took hearts deep into the primeval timber,
where crimes of passion run thickest, where the royal
stag's eye stares back, a glimpse at death in your soul.

Waifs

Wanting home before dark, my wife and I
travel south dredging the Virginia piedmont.
She marvels at the charcoal scape outside:
Amish oxen browse yoked together, several
Airstreamers docked on rims scar from rust.
Counting the spidery fenceposts, she reaches
one sporting the crude sign: "No Fishing."
"Where do the children play?" my wife asks.

From their beds they steal away to the farm
pond. Wading out, the sneaky waifs catch
black fish to conceal beneath their coats.
They creep back up the hill, quietly
inside the farmer's house, thinking the night is yet
young when only old men fall asleep. The waifs draw
straws to decide what prize to leave:
fish are stashed upright in the medicine cabinet.

III
Places

White Trash in Summer

After his filibuster, our cleric recesses mid-day Mass; I
cease swatting his lordly flies, pass without blessing
myself, and dash out to watch the breezy sundresses
of Catholic girls whose cold numbers are best suited for
looking. I loosen my collar, tug at my necktied lust, start
my Chevy rolling through the piedmont, flaring its
fins and scoop, running its nose down, chewing up
leagues of slab hot and black as Satan's tattooed whore.
I drive casing the countryside where my father's people
cultivated burley tobacco for Mister R. J. Reynold's scions.
I mull it over taking the thick Cuban cigar stuck behind the visor,

smoke my way past the fields and farms banging my grill home—
God's dewy acre of a truck garden, narrow daybed, a brick
privy. I pass the rosebud steeple, where I know Baptists'
fiery throats sing; the doors fling wide, spilling
the goers who spraddle on sheets, lunch pails burst
open for a feast. I lean far out the window, discerning
a certain girl's lilting laughter, glimpse her eyes blue
as the Madonna's robes I see captured in stained glass.
I seethe over my thwarted love and lack of balls to have her.
All June I've paced night carpets, wanting her in my dreams,
but I can't go behind my father's fear of snake-worship
to pebble her shut panes. Summer shakes the worst in me;
I rumble past the white trash, pumping my tin horn for love.

Winter Fields: Getting Through

This morning the melancholia
you posed makes a sort of sense: February
can get awfully, awesomely blue.
But here past the dim rock wall,
the hoarfrost shellacking left last
night creates a loveliness surpassing
that of snowfall. I breathe deep downy

silence; the early morning breeze plays
a scherzo, shaking the shaggy trees.
Twiggy fists of crystals shatter. Limbs
tremble at the increasing tempo of wind;
veils and streamers shower me. Powders
catapult, collapse from the evergreens.
The air of sudden becomes alive with snow-music.
Then all of note is finished. Hemlocks
unburdened: I trudge homeward.

Building a Fencerow

After Arbor Day the evening air grows
sharp and painfully cold; out back our
property I chunk the posthole digger
through brick-mire, sparks from the metal biting
cherts. Lantern on the El Dorado's flipped
down tailgate sputters, shaking out shadows
of a giant knocking sticks and switches
off a cedar log with a hatchet, chipping
blunt noses to set in holes. What a dog-
sired job with no neighbors to spell
me for a shot of Southern Comfort. Car doors
ajar look like batwings as the push
button radio plays Luke the Drifter's
seventy-eights; a soldier courts his dream
girl on the banks of the old Pontchartrain
Lake. I bury the axe blade in the marrow of a stump,
tug on my fleeced coat, head for the house,
and you holding me near whisper, "You smell
like winter coming on soon this year."

Catching a Flick in Morelia

Tonight's wet moviegoers loiter
closeby the curbstone, hunched and hatless
trolls. Ten pesos I peel off to face a
forgettable flick I caught earlier at
the matinee. Under the roof we file,
blinking in the reefer darkness, conspirators
huddled together to watch the Pathé
newsreels sport Wrong Way Culligan and his funny
flying machine, building hype to *The Lime Twig*.
The big picture plugs its credits,
fingering the gaffers, but I miss the script
hacks responsible for this mess. Tugging
out a sock wadded with figs, I chew
deciphering subtitles worded in screwy Portugese,
sit charmed wondering how the hell does an
expatriate down here teach film to blind
mice holed up in the barrios amongst their exquisite
filth? Whose practical sense of high art
derives from the twisted Mayan totems leering
about subterranean lobbies where it's not uncommon
for those in a stew to ride the rails all goddamn night.

Getting Mad and Even

You watched out for them, or else
you got coldcocked by those voodoo
maulers who were never shy to wing
any pitch they could muscle headlong at you:
A barber's sharp curve, breaking high, tight,
shaving your mustache; a mean slider
fixing to knock out your knees; junkballs
snaking off your socks. This sport licensed
blood and you were game. You planted your
stance in the batter's box and mustered your
truest whacks at the hairy grenades they
lobbed off the mound triggering their battery
mates to laugh behind your ears at the hilarity
of it all. Soon your nerves crawled
along edges for cutting, guessing with a wry smile
they'd next uncork the widowmaker: a beanball
pegged for your blanched temples. And you dived,
dived all the way to the bruising turf, ass
busted in lime and spit, getting up rickety, not unshaken,
plotting with the war club clenched in your fists.

If He Hollers, Let Him Go

Ferris Fain's defunct now you know,
I found his obituary beneath Thursday's box
scores. I suppose he's gone off to meet
up with Terry and the Pirates we last read at sea
aboard burning decks. Anymore Fain's done shagging
Cuban heels, flicking stogies into gashouse
brawls, and forever goosing the organ-grinder's
monkey. Ferris, the kid was all heart: in his
book scooting down a bunt was outrageous, a friendly
slap on the ass was "fag's stuff." He bowed his
legs like a wishbone, faced the Pale Hose, took
licks that could bring hail, or else he stuffed
satchels for the Sally League. All along his sophomore
summer, he rode the jinx long enough to cap the batting
championship by early September. Job finished, he
trained far south to run a service station, peddling
Esso gas and rat poison, all the winter muscles
yelling play ball. Yet each March brought around
the sooty thumbs to fetch him north to Pittsburgh
where of late the madder he grew to think he'd busted
his aging chops for God's paying zoo. After he retired
his numbers from the sport, any yen to come from behind
back the bleachers was alleviated. I'd buck odds in this
morning's post that the A's front office received
a card, simply put: "Bring me back now, you SOB's."

Mail at My New Address

This rented flat in New Orleans offers a cat's
view where I watch through wavy panes
ancient trolleys squeaking along the Soo Line.
Peering from behind the burgundy begonias
potted yesterday, I smell their musty peat
when I squat on the windowsill. Bad-bellied

clouds blow free I swear to drench the whole
quarter like a soaked glove. I've mapped my
plans here beside the storm sash and, hell, why
not? At seventy-three looking doesn't hurt;
it humors a shut-in soul who otherwise has day
long to read campy crime novels, sling chalk at
wrens bickering on the red rooftops and file his

nails across the chewed grips glued to a cheap gun.
The postman arrives, humpbag bulging, tramping
through the drizzle. He stands beneath the awning,
shakes out his canvas wrap like a rheumy duck then
squats to sift through Christmas mail. He thinks it
queer nothing gets to this new address. He doesn't
know it has been days since I've written anything.

Hanging Gardens

The hanging gardens cultivated at Xochimilco
I know now are neither, it's an outright lie: the itinerate
student pays freight far south to view the floral
terraces, learns nothing lush grows there except scrim
lilies, bobbing like cowdung plastered on the waterways.
Pink carp ply the fetid canals; their saw-toothed
fins scrape the bottoms of your feet through the dinghy.
Up ahead the girl who'll begin Grinnell in the fall
politely chatters in Spanish, how pretty are your gardens,
while she perspires and wilts. Breathe the peevish air
deep enough in this tropical gutter, and you'll get back
burning at both ends, heir to the sleeping sickness.
I shudder at a passing ague of vertigo, fret about
falling faint, rely on mariachis to dredge me from
the sump, undone before smelling the fabled orchids.
Each day this trip grows more insane. I detect
signs in the streets others fail to notice: swarthy
boys tethered behind butcher stalls sling slurs like
gleaming knives uncloaked in catlight. Going without
sleep, I'll get up to breakfast on seltzer, bent
on catching, hell yes, catching the tin stork home.

Little Haiti

In my hometown Haiti Street spills
downslope the courthouse; I seldom travel
that way: Haiti is meant for blue evenings
I look to step outside my lonely biography.
The luminary clock glowers straightup for
evening meal, housemothers hush clattering
dishes, tap out six chimes, resume setting
clabber and snapbeans on the table. Out front
the terrace, bickering children invent play.
Hydrangea blooms alongside the railing, a
seamstress scolds after the girls, "Come, comb
my hair. Come soothe my riled nerves." Girls climb
the grade to the library lending them the marvelous
story of how cool and correct Toussaint L'Ouverture
led his fighting tigers to drive the demon-
Frenchmen from the islands. Today Haitian girls
stroll the streets singing his name: Toussaint,
Toussaint, Toussaint L'Ouverture. Their
chorus brings his ghosts to haunt my
hometown, shaking the treetops.

Not Out of the Woods

I tramped inside with the shouldered weight
of a .243, its breech filled to kill blue-blooded
stags who ventured off the ridge to lick salts.
Drowsy, I sang the sun to crack at the east's far
temples. Deep inside those woods I knew lay the
tumbled masonry of stone fence, where I
squatted for breath and tippled bombay gin.
I studied the naked aspect of the quiet forest,
with the colors to summer's coat bleeding, the leaves
drifting as clefs, their dry notes heard on spongy
compost beneath the balls of my feet. In early
November my false passion to stalk deer flared,
and once I shot, after being shot at. No, for me
the sport was derived for figuring the mystery an
abandoned rock wall begged. A lonely hunter came
along, perhaps. In the dim lateness of day he confused
his moorings for the while and happened here
upon what he took as a property line. He leaned
his gnarled fowling piece against a trunk, slumped
into a drunken sleep, and with the settling night,
dreamt how the fence steered him out of the woods.

Caution Lights

Amid that carnival season, I wager she knew damn
well that the honeysuckle's fug hanging in the air
would heighten those muggy, tarry nights in the
erotic. Offhours we climbed the garret like two
naked ghosts and slipped beneath the storm sash,

steptoeing down the red slate as we'd before.
There the whole upstairs of space mattered only
ours to see, the sky looking as though in passing
a drunken giant had stumbled, his cheroot dashed,
its embers spattering into a velvet map of constellations.

Legs spraddled on my wrap, her eyes seemed to grow
vague, veiled: Kissing her kewpie doll was screwy.
Her old man rolled in his lounge, thinking the unspelled
rapping he heard on top the tiles were stray cats in love.
Her damn eyes and hooks are what undid me, what with

fumbling clingy and damp cloth, and I almost hiked
the chemise off her shoulders. Nearby the nervy tops
of trees switched in the salt breeze off the Gulf;
I turned to look east, toward the blood-orange glow of
a radio tower flickering its caution lights at me.

41

Little Boy Blue

North from Heron, looking for redneck
pheasants flushed out of corn stubble, I
first glimpse the blue sleeves flapping in
the Christmas wind. Turning back, I slowly
approach the figure, wishing it a clay
mummy. Hair grows on the little knuckles
instead. A cloaked child has fallen dead to
me. Pathologists tell me the body is bathed
in rich mineral salts, has perfect milk
teeth and healthy bones. There's no inkling
of foul play. His face I remember peacefully
sleeping, abandoned by his keepers. Lost on
a highway beneath the cold Nebraska stars they
wept, gently laid the lad to rest, his hands
put over his heart. Since in my dreams, I watch
the Christ child naked, crying in straw and the
hot vapor of stable beasts. Stumbling outside,
as far off I can see, are miles of hoary fields where
nothing even on a prayer lives through the night.

Something Wrong
(for Kenneth Patchen)

You must have sensed her painted young sisters
before hawking under the red glare of gas
lights pulsing like an artery, their coiled
snake bangles clinking together from the illicit
motion of putting a hand on your folded arm:
"Buddy, help me get this trick." Her voice
veered among the poles of the erotic and forlorn,
tightening your throat like a tourniquet. A drench
swept in drumming on the steamy pavement;
the stopped cab's headlights writing something wrong
on the rain, all about this evening. Dry and sitting
later inside a clean-swept Latin cabaret, a smoke
after coffee, she leaned over to kiss in your ear
why she wanted so badly to leave town that lonely
night. Out of the rain you understood her thought:
laughing like Mary and Magdalene, she said money
mattered little now and she licensed your groping hands
to slide between those adolescent thighs like razors.
You didn't ask her if she'd ever been in love before.

Summons to Enigma

On edge of spring's foul clime my father's
people cabled me for a hasty summons to Enigma,
hamlet I swore never to breathe in again, unless in
the gleeful event its gardens were laced with salt;
its vital vinegar works went belly-up; its one
cathouse grieved over a venereal pox which would

curdle the bones of each backdoor cracker in town.
It seemed the beetle-legged gent took a vicious
kick in the kidneys brought by drinking bootjack
that could knock Moses blind, reeling in the painted
desert, howling at devils. "Blood of your blood,"
came the Freewill Baptists' ado that I didn't need to
hear now standing at the ledge, peering down the earthy,

clammy excavation. Was it whole enough to swallow
an old man's bile during his later days? I thought
riding home. Bad feelings know no bounds,
and the melancholy seldom lifts much, but you do go on.
Knocking at the gabled manse of hyacinths. Meeting
faces I'd missed at the dark station. Returning to
fetch carnie queens, tan and wet. Such form the pictures
which shutter your senses while at a wake in Enigma.

IV
Biography

Fallen Angel
(for Weldon Kees)

Fog's all right. Those angels who fall
through the air without wings won't kick
if it comes: they often laugh, talking
about their borrowed ration of time.
They wear protective clothing:
wet suit, wrestling shoes, life-preserver.
High-diving from the bridge, they attempt
to land feet first; the wind flips
them on their backs. Death is quick.

Fog's all right. One angel's fate remains
conjectural then. Speaking of both
suicide and retiring abroad under
an assumed name, his blue De Soto
was found beneath the stacked heels
of Golden Gate Bridge. Beyond the window,
I think of him north in a few
lighted rooms of that ruined house,
a candle in each open pane of breath.

Teeth of the Hydra

One evening Edward Teach
prowled these cold waters.
His grackle eyes marveled
how the moon spread her apron,
carving clumsy scrimshaw,
the waves breaking adventurers'

backs on the reef. He drank rum
mixed with gunpowder; spitting
out the flame, he pistol
whipped his messmates.

He dried their bones on a white beach,
cast their skulls in molten gold:
Circe demanded macabre
purses. Teach met her
in dark fog, the scarf of gold skulls

alive and breathing around
her throat. She pressed
a teacup to her clay lips,
watching the leaves settle.
"Come here,
Come here, Blackbeard."
His soul crept from the teacup.

At the Moon's Gate

Charles V anointed his fiery hidalgo to furl
sail, break lances for Christ, subdue the King's
pagan gardens. There de Soto squandered his youth,
whoring pliant squaws and fleecing royal mines. He
wintered his last beneath bright, loco moons. Once
moonstruck, the manic captain stalked past scalp poles
to ruin his raw animal robes and his young Chickasaw

bride both to serve his King's new house, not chaste
but carnal. The lush maize grew as a yellow ore, perhaps
what the Crown lusted after, but the starving Spaniards
stole for its food substance. The fabled string pearls
and ingots late of Cuzco, de Soto dreamt gleamed nearby
in the fairy forest: "The amber sap, how it overflows
His chalice!" De Soto's legions sprawled in a pauper's
stupor at the Moon's Gate, far from their ghostly galleons.

"O black Sabbath," wailed the priest crawling naked
to purge his pale flesh with ashes and bitter wine.
'Flee at once from this land!" "Never," the Adelantado
hissed. "I feast as Lucifer's sister in gold." April's
cruel end, de Soto splashed upon yellow springs of River
Mississippi to die. Yanked on a yew stake in full amor,
de Soto slipped to a quagmire grave. The mute sergeant
banged his drum: "It's the playing of the madman's tide."

The Strange Case of Doctor Mudd

A smackwater physician, remedying
megrims with foul smelling salts,
I perched inside my oakshade
magdalene here on the Northern Neck, a far
wail from the field hospitals bleeding
my dreams dry. I laughed at the satirical
cartoons charcoaled in London's *Punch*
depicting the angular rube, maul
poised in fists, splintering rails into duff.

During the winter, I whored along the wharves
in Baltimore, meeting Wilkes inside a stew.
We droned on as a pair of conspiratorial crows,
agreeing how the war was wrongly askew
for Richmond; copperheads filled only with
hissing failed to win battles: desperate
measures were needed by April. What
occurred in the ensuing days, I left to Lew
Wallace and his toadies' conjecture; I swore
that I never knew "Tyson" and "Tyler" who

came to my house, Tyler injured in a fall
off his horse. Was I to leave the man
to suffer? I set his lame leg, and they slept
upstairs; in the morning they left by the cornfield,
entering Zekiah marsh, Tyler wearing false whiskers,
a tatty shawl, and a brace of handsome horse
pistols. Four years I walked the lonesome
beaches at Dry Tortugas, combing for miniature
shells to assemble a jewelry case. Pardoned,
health wrecked, I stay now in Havana, old before
fifty, taking to my grave an untold story.

Hôpital Albert Schweitzer

i

Fulgent moon springs the bocors, the island
witch doctors, masquerading in the negro streets
as sapphire wasps whose painterly wings tinge
pestilence in the village with an uncanny voodoo.
Inside their mud huts, tar babies teethe on sticky sorghum,
mothers squat by dung fires to cook rice and red
beans, curse the judas priests promising outright
to heal and all the while bleeding you turnip poor.

ii

Portered by litter, the lame cross the quag
God gave to Cain: they assemble to wait out
front the Hôpital, pipesmoking sinsemilla
beneath the giant mapou tree. A lightfooted child
climbs far up its chalky and spraddled limbs. She
melts candle snubs dug in the bark; warm wax
drips down onto the footway like fallen notes,
calling out benevolent ghosts from inside the tree.

iii

The diesel generator turns on, keeping the bulbs
hung in the morning wards alive: here summer's
jaundice festers and dies. The sick sleep on
biafran cots and stumble into dreams: icy water
flumes down from the mountains in deep aqueducts.
Pungent night orchids seep through the shut louvers.
Baby-green iguanas scurry along volcanic ledges
where a child pelts them with stones that don't break.

Honeycutt Goes Iron

He burned the honey locust rails
his grandfather had timbered to
erect around the family cemetery plot.
The hard wood smoldered for days,
thick as salt crust on the old man's
cheeks, not of sponge. He built
a new fence of wrought iron,
the pikes pointing inward toward
the field stones, carved simply:
"Honeycutt." Neighbors say the old
man's ghost clangs his broadax
on the wrought iron fence.

Mrs. Lincoln Enters Bellevue Place

Ten o'clock Pliny Earle my own physician
administers chloral drops, then the Indian
ghost returns to lift my scalp and unhook
again the banjo strings behind my eyes.
When I hear other voices trapped between
the walls, the quack scribbles in his ledger:

a debility of the nervous system. Rest
comes when I dream of wintering this year
quietly among the limes and oranges, left
alone to concentrate my mind wonderfully,
embracing the kiss of kin as if still near.
It is the drudgery of this modern management

of mental disease by morphia, ale, croquet,
monitored menstrual flow and fresh air I so
long to divorce. Ninety sleepy miles by
freight from Chicago, Robert visits on a lawyer's
Wednesday afternoons when we walk, arms linked,

in the yellow wood. He brings me crinoline,
grieves I suspect for not taking me, but our
little experiment caused him to break housekeeping
to end the troubles I brewed with his wife. At night
when the moon slips as spirits across my pillow, I smell
all of those red orchids pressed between Scripture and dream.

Mrs. Lincoln Winters in Nice

Retiring from the last song tonight, I think of
all those trunks beneath the rafters, left
locked at 373 Pacific, keepsakes in autistic
storage: I care for none of these things, the red
velvet you must have the mulatto seamstress
stitch into the dress for your lovely looks in the
evening. Russian fur sewn on the collar
becomes you, child-bride of my son, with
a matched muffler to warm your fine-china doll's
hands. A widow's life has so changed me: do
pack the President's private effects and remove
them by rail to your vacant guest's bedchamber.
Your husband will want to remember to sort out
the wools and lace them in camphor, wrap them
with Chicago's yellow tabloids. I live with a
holy terror of moths chewing raggedy blotches through
my wear. The Jewish doctor applied his tube to
my sore lungs and pronounced me unfit to winter
hereabouts. I suppose I will wander south, looking
for a drier climate. Italy, perhaps. I keep
a box of 12 colognes concealed for you, how
provoking you should not have it — at this time.
It will do for the next. My eyes droop for the want
of sleep which never comes; a moth flutters closeby
the candlelight, its singed wings snuff out the wick
and the room goes dark and you will read the last from me.

53

All Her Pretty Ones
(Sussex, 1941)
(for Virginia Woolf)

Never in her worst nightmares had she
dared to imagine that the Earth's
axis would turn on itself again, in a
fury of dog madness. To snuff out all
her pretty ones, those stalwart lads
beneath the shade at Kew, fresh out of royal
academies, conscripted to fight as vile
moles, coughing the gas of the Antichrist.

She climbs up again to the lofty ledge and
stands watching the surf break against the
black rocks. Looking across the English
Channel, she's anxious for news from France.
She extends her shaky fingers, as if touching
ghosts, westerly across the sea to the colonies,
summoning the giant who sleeps. The ermine collar

alive and breathing around her throat becomes
illuminated in a spurt of sulphur, embraced
by the reassurance of blue smoke wreaths.
How deep, how numb the dark sea? Those
wartime phantom voices keep recurring here,
high on the chalk cliffs overlooking lethal
jetties. She shudders at the Nazi shadows
high over London. Clarions bleat. Firespit bombs
descend. What voice within her follows the tide?

Portrait of the Outlaw

See him in the Bosporus sailing beneath the fire
gem stars, not yet 18, lulled to drifting
by the slapping surf, carving mahogany scrimshaw, nights
dreaming male dreams of God's pliant
angel-whores and jeweled jungle idols, of exotic
southerly islands in jade seas. "Men of science

forgive these poor painters who have forever
remained children," the broker penned to his rogue
mistress. Slumming in Paris he painted a coy
young girl sitting boldly naked in a bright blue
throne beside her orange monkey. Life remained a fete
even into his vesper years when Paul dared to portray
his mother as virgin. See the hoary painter in his

"House of Pleasure": rats gnawing at the thatch roof,
sores on his legs bleeding, erotica stirring about
his pallet. Did Gauguin die of morphine, a glass heart,
tropical syphilis? The outlaw bequeathed to scholars to
bicker over the fatal vision he couldn't commit to
his canvas found flapping in the Tahitian breezes.

How Peter Lorre Could Have Saved My Life

I suppose because it was the Mardi Gras
and I got a little stoned on peyote;
I expected the dog-faced reincarnation
of Peter Lorre to appear fumbling at
broken door chimes, puffing his polite

snort of rye and bringing news about my
ex-mistress who resided in a flat off
Bourbon Street where reeked dark opiates,
perfumes, and our sinful excesses. ("How she
leeched me ill.") Perhaps it was the carnival
madness, but I wanted out from the conjurer

who was rumored of lying with swine and worse
consorting with Circe. I'd bribe Mr. Lorre
and the French police to rake her into a snake
pit, seek asylum in a Mercedes and beat it Mexico
bent down the coast, peyote wind stirring crazy
my locks. But tonight Lorre never knocked — she did.

Trout Fishing

Loblolly shack and out back a trout
stream is floating away through evening's
hushed drizzle. I knock the red mud off
my boots and slip indoors to open
your blue blouse, warming my cold
coarse hands on your bare breasts. You
laugh and shudder aside from the battering
fillets, served snow-white off the ebony
woodstove. We beat back the clock when all
at once it's night time, a few moments alone
sipping wine, our young bodies leaning closer.
Drifting asleep, I hear the trout and stream
trickle over wishes we'll grow old together.

The Tobacco Queen

All summer I knew that he was intently
watching me, stooping in yellow tobacco,
August sun warming my tanned arms and bare
shoulders. Hired man, he bedded in the barn
loft, his oil lamp flickering well past starry
midnights. From the apron of the field, I
paused under the mingo tree, myself in turn
eyeing the blonde satan picking the burly sheaths
to pack uphill to the cure shed. Prize tobacco
to market, we'd give the help cash and send him on.

I slipped the latch key and stole near the bright
bonfires, spitting sparks. The thirsty, sweet fug
of curing tobacco so like bodies sharing love flared
my nostrils and I called out to his trancy shadows.
We became wild in the semi-dark, his raw mouth
and hands, tasting of maduro, roving my breasts as silk
spun from evening spiders. Leaning over my face,
his thumbs smoothed my cheekbones, making me endure
the burning tobacco. He traced the glow, whispering:
"You, you're the Tobacco Queen." Then he was gone.

About the Author

Edward C. Lynskey was born in 1956 and grew up near Washington, D. C. and in the piedmont region of Virginia. A graduate of George Mason University, he received his M. A. from there in 1984. He currently teaches advanced composition at George Mason University and works as a senior technical writer in the defense industry. His fiction, reviews, and poetry have appeared nationwide in such journals as *The Atlantic Monthly, American Poetry Review, The New York Times, Washington Post, San Francisco Chronicle, Carolina Quarterly, America, Virginia Quarterly Review, College English, Cleveland Plain Dealer, Southern Poetry Review, Prairie Schooner, Southern Humanities Review* and *Southwest Review*. His previous poetry volumes are *Wrought Iron* (Northern Virginia Community College, 1980) and *Teeth of the Hydra* (Crop Dust Press, 1986). *The Tree Surgeon's Gift* was a finalist in the 1987 Virginia Prize for Poetry. A fourth manuscript *Mrs. Lincoln Winters in Nice* is expected for publication in early 1991.

Scripta Humanistica

Directed by
BRUNO M. DAMIANI
The Catholic University of America
COMPREHENSIVE LIST OF PUBLICATIONS *

BOOK ORDERS

* Clothbound. *All book orders*, except library orders, must be prepaid and addressed to **Scripta Humanistica**, 1383 Kersey Lane, Potomac, Maryland 20854. *Manuscripts* to be considered for publication should be sent to the same address.